DESIRE PRISM

Desire Prism

Maia Spring Carabajal

2025

Desire Prism
By Maia Spring Carabajal
2025

Copyright Maia Spring Carabajal 2025.
The moral rights of the author have been asserted.
All rights reserved.

Revised January 2026.

Contents

1. *How To Disappear* — 9
2. *I Saw Us Old* — 11
3. LSD — 13
4. *You Were A Jim Harrison* — 17
5. 01012016 — 19
6. *I Miss Your Body Next To My Body* — 23
7. *As For Writers* — 25
8. *Blue* — 29
9. *Initiations* — 33
10. JG — 35
11. 12292016 — 39
12. *Woman* — 41
13. *Sun* — 43
14. *It Is Not Art* — 45
15. *I Do Not Love You Today* — 49
16. *Chiron* — 51
17. *Orpheo Looks Back* — 53
18. *Crown and Anchor Me* — 55
19. *Silence* — 57
20. *Catharsis* — 61
21. *I Want To Love You More Than Poetry* — 63
22. *When He Finds Her* — 65
23. *How You Are* — 67
24. *Asking A Stranger* — 69
25. *So Many Singers* — 71
26. *I Don't Know What To Say* — 73
27. *The Brightness* — 77

28.	*Intimacy*	79
29.	*Cave*	81
30.	*12072019*	83
31.	*12082019*	85
32.	*Magdalene*	87
33.	*In The End Everything Is Simple*	89
34.	*Each Cell Is A Poem*	91
35.	*Twilight*	93
36.	*Intact*	95
37.	*My Soul Is Hungry For You*	97
38.	*My Grief Is Not Simple*	99
39.	*Guest*	101
40.	*Dressing A Wound*	105
41.	*My Grief Is Sacred*	107
42.	*Content In Ordinary Love*	109
43.	*Blue Eyed Soul*	111
44.	*Everything Now*	113
45.	*Maps*	115
46.	*Discovered You*	117
47.	*Habits*	119
48.	*Lament*	121
49.	*Song*	123
50.	*Prometheus*	125
51.	*Anniversary*	129
52.	*Why?*	131
53.	*In This Place*	133
54.	*Tell Me*	135
55.	*Aaron*	137
56.	*Good*	139
57.	*Phantom Limb*	141

| 58. | *Heavy* | 143 |
| 59. | *We Are Lived By Everything That We Love* | 145 |

How To Disappear

I have learned to fear less than violence.
I know the insidious nature
of thick silence that conceals wishes.

I can disappear.
Evaporate like
fleeting recollections of preference.

Slow erosion of opinion
that shows faint
through worn fabric of a shallow life.

I will to starvation.
To to arrive at emptiness.
I slip like whispers thin as ghosts
from room to room.

Fending off tears divined
from the only emotion I sympathize with.
Longing for a promise taken for granted.

When the vulnerable become disappointed
they revoke their magic.
All numb to hide in an artful shelter
of invisibility.

Common sadness no longer moves me.
I cry for those who recoil in fetal loneliness.
A static bitterness permeates regress.

The remaining hues that show through
dense gray, black, white
are blue of steel guitar strings
or amber of subdued anger.

The soup sits
cold and unconsumed.
As steam rises
into a frozen sky
of new betrayal.

I Saw Us Old

He was moving slowly
toward a seat at a restaurant table.
I wanted to grab him by the elbows
to help him sit.
His legs were shaking.
His back was curved.
I turned away
with impatient agony.

The woman with him smiled.
Her content gaze rested easeful
into the lines of her face.
I thought she must have been
fifteen years younger than him.

What were they to each other.
He braving a Friday evening downtown.
Her limber, luminous, baring no anxiety.
She paced slowly behind his every movement.
Attentive, undisturbed.

Was she daughter,
niece, lover,
nurse or cousin.

I observed them in ambiguous celebration.
I thought one day we might be like this.

LSD

He lamented fearing psychosis.
Being taken by nature.
Consumed by dæmonic constellation.
Neurons, synapses, transmitters:
turning, moving into uncommon shapes.
Mind-spinning dropping the mood
into lysergic acid diethyl amide midnight.

He fears what he is curious of.
Poking, prodding, stroking
the Westerner's great beast.
Timid that rapport
may not have been maintained.

All those years
rolling, rotating, holding.
straining it through his fingers.
Rough sketches, wet paintings.
Almost making love to it.

Mine comes like a golden smog.
A breath of sunset that takes my stride,
observes my aloneness.
Embraces my vision, my body.
Floods my shadow.
Making it all too warm,
too connected.

Madness strings the detail of life together.
A golden thread collecting tiny glass beads,

offering strands.
Tempting me with symmetry.

Coincidence, harmony, paranoia
slide on top of each other.
A lens of concentric circles
through which the world
is a rose hued horror.

A toast to madness—
to anyone's preferred sin.
To the twelve PM vodka.
To the borderline flood
of rocking passion.
The ascetic starvation.

The waiting.
The counting.
The tapping.

Momentum for the sake
of momentum.

The hermetically sealed prison
we make of our lives.

The room.
The market.
The park.
The highway.

A toast to the safety valve
that mitigates each dispersion

one
drop
at a
time.

You Were A Jim Harrison

I begged not to
and dreamed of your ruddy skin.
A tapestry of inflammation,
of sunburn,
of pocked landmarks.
Your whiskey lips
and liver large,
a second bosom.

I begged not to
and remembered
your thick blonde chest
against my cheek
in the morning
with puppy sweet talk.
Promises of intricate letters
mapping the heart of things.
Licked, stamped and sent off
across three towns.
Traveling your shore to my city.

The distance is tepid and serene.
I can speak across it
as if I were reciting prose.
You can dictate to me
which lines are poetry
and which are stagnant deepities.

Full of gin and breaking
the silence of my works.

Delivering them
one after another
after another.

Our works are houses we hide inside of.
We covet each other's property.

Held up in some corner booth.
In some warmly lit bar
blessed with privacy.
You were a Jim Harrison.
I was a no-name poet.

Not quite a Nin.
Wondering what my work could mean.
Wondering what your heart could mean.

With hands deep in the chill
of our separate sleep.
I have not called our answered
except in the ice of that dream.

Our movement swept
until the floorboards
coughed woodgrain.

We are shallow pools of champagne.
Half-written letters to synthetic saviours.

01012016

FOR ELIZABETH MOORE

Following me anywhere
along this curve,
spiral, snap.
A jerking storyline.
Her car winds around
the mid-divide.

She is more grey.
She was like this before.
I could not yet see it.

I will tear you apart,
she gushes with conviction.
All I want is for them is to grow
once I leave them.

They flounder,
tread water.
Calling from inside a well.
Surrounded,
taken by the echo chamber.

I hide the poems I wrote
two summers,
three summers past.
Speaking into the void
with simple language.

I hold the moments she saw anarchy

with awes tremendous space.
Hoping the temperature drop
will guide us out of the tension
we learned in glorious play.

It won't shut off.
The tiny fridge buzzes.
The small room fills
with our endless
cigarette smoke.

We are not leaving.

I am not leaving her.
Not until the sun comes up
and I am no longer the young woman
I was when we first met.

Not until I've regretted mind's sleep
and the laziness of my hands
when his heart was too heavy to carry.

Only once I have latched on
to enough of her storm.

We are twelve, four, seven, twenty-two:
remembering mother love.
We are sixty remembering
mothering our mothers.

Fear merely an alarm bell
a trusted hound
growling at the front door.
Anger, a furnace

generator propelling us
tempered with grace.

Guilt.
Shame — avoided
respectively.

And love — illusive.

Our separate gravities
and magnetism
repelling each other.

Once she was the only one.
So was I.

For a little while
we are true friends
again.

I Miss Your Body Next To My Body

I miss your body next to my body.
I woke this morning to a memory.
I turned to find your face and eyes.
My arms almost reached for you.
My dry fingers
nearly caressed your warm hand.

My lips twitched and quivered
as they readied to give you a greeting kiss.

Two kisses.
One for your cheek.
One for your mouth.

Two kisses, to say,
hello, welcome.

I realized that you were not there.
I woke into Lorca's memory.

Some dead poet who knew love better than I.
I miss your body next to mine.

As For Writers

Months in retrograde.
Reaching backward.
Setting charts.
Documenting each lover,
failure, success.

I learned to love myself
when I could not write.
Then mastered how to gauge
the flood of inspiration.

I learned to stop life.
To dam. Omit.
Refrain from celebration.

Some mornings I woke
swarming with words.
Some words I wrote.
Some I ignored.

I learned to theorize about the act
when silence fell upon my life.
I learned to write about writing
when there were no concepts
to summon or keep at bay.

I appreciated sitting outside of madness.
Bypassing trite themes.
Observed similar characters
walking on and off of stages.

I learned to succumb to the archetypal drama.

Understood what it requires
to live a life well documented.
To take a life down onto paper.
Learned the rhythms.
Sensing when to pick up the pen.
When to set it down.

To not ignore the muse when she calls.
To miss her like an absent mother.
To long for her.
To summon her.
To cry for her.
To be indifferent toward her.

We have chosen an art.
One that takes a magnifying glass
to the threads that stitch our lives together.
Cutting along the seams.
Examining the mind.
The heart. The body.

The movements of nature.
The dance of the living,
The dance of the dead.

We are drunk.
We are sober.
We are present.

We are peering into
and passing through
revolving dimensions.

We have learned
to set out the time for introspection.
To go into the impulse.
The trigger.

Examining the matter and immaterial.
Revealing the self to the self.
Revelling in the shifting boundary
between self and other.
Whole and particle.
Tribe and individual.

Students
of the romantic,
the real.

This is how we've lived.
In the depth and in the shallows.
In the plastic, the plasticity,
and the stubborn.

In the fantasy
and in the freezing chrome
of indifference.

Systematic dedication to the process
of allowing the whole of being
to run through the hand and onto the page.
Run through the page and into print.
Through print and into the microphone.
Through the amp and into the crowd.

For the observance of quint celebration.
For the small gratitude in connection.

It is as if my life was not my own.

It is as if the love, the static, the heat
are shared themes activated for the stanza.

Living for the letter.
Living for the line.
That dies when unsung.

Blue

I seek in your flesh the tracks of my lips.

I mumble a line that I want to be mine
but it's Lorca's.

Are you still painting?
What made your art beautiful.
What made me scrape each metaphor backward
back into the notebooks that I call my best work.

I think your name.
Afterward
I mutter
I love you.

A prayer folds
into the hum of a public bus
squeezing through grey buildings.
I try to string soft words together
but remember
that I have become someone
you would not read.

Each syllable is a filler vowel.

Each metaphor redundant like: house.
Like: body.
Like: tree.
Like: veins.
Like: gold.

Like: like.

I want to dream magic again.
To anticipate the resonance of auras
as we sit feet apart.
Never touching,
Imagining that there are scriptures
beneath a third layer of skin.

We read by the precision of intuitions scalpel.
We read by the dim light of a damned god.

There are no more stanzas.
Only flat prose.
Stifled yawns.

I seek in my flesh the tracks of your—
I borrow someone else's madness.

I edit six years of a belief in art.

Six hundred pages of an attempt
to get face-to-face with illusion.

To get underneath the facade.
To stroke the unconscious.
Finger her gently
until she does my bidding.

Discovering only redundant metaphors.
Like: body.
Like: tree.
Like: veins.
Like: gold.

Like: like.

I go back to witness
playing games of hide and seek.
Folding truth into dull language.
That cannot unlock.
That obscures
the sustained passion
of a decade
of a belief in art.

I rewrite each poem
side by side
using them
the way I used your name.
Scraping each phrase backwards
against another page
to scour again for meaning.

Are you still writing.

I seek in your flesh the tracks your—

On a pin's point my love is—

Initiations

He taught me how to walk gently.
To set my spine and clear akashic records
within a set of breathes.

I knew of emptiness.
Reading Siddhartha, Lao Tzu.
Then took on the blackness of morphine
and a granted wish for death.

He taught me how to touch
without touching.
To mend without a needle.
To cut with no scalpel.

I could disappear.
Journey through the fluid.
Journey through the plasma.
Become the body
of another.

I lived this way.
Meditating on the void
until I had made
one thousand promises
to speak in whispers.
To set things back
the way they sat
before I came.
To serve the intention of the other.

Meditating into eternities.
Years became decades.
Decades of initiations.
One thousand promises
made to an absent god.

Promises made
to dead prophets.

A set of rites.
A set of instructions
on how to journey
through the fluid.
Journey through the plasma.
Become the body of another.

One thousand promises.
To speak in whispers.
To sit at the table.
To set the original face.
To guide atoms back
to the way there were
before our meeting was conceived.

One thousand promises.
To serve the intention
of the other.

JG

Send them back in.
Single file.

Chained to images
of those they cannot compare.

One arrives with the first awakening.
Accidentally stumbling upon enlightenment.

Another wears his families crest.
A four leaf clover.
Boasting of the way his blood takes to Pilsner
and the gut to estrogen.

Another takes a stroll down to the red brick corner
where he gives his best political speech
to the addicts huddled beneath scaffolding
off Broadway and 9th St.

I must inspect them.
Every cavity.
As if I am playing Doctor.
Playing house.
Playing sister.
Playing mother.

Every question
a perfect script.

And I am bored.

Too accustomed
to the coming
and going.
To the narrative of introduction.
To the silence between notes.

No, Darling.
I would not leave you angry.
I would not give you the satisfaction
of feeling despair,

Despair is yet another reason
to sink further
into the comfortable hell.

The pounding of molten things.
The slickness of shame.
The heat of jealousy.

I should leave. I should leave.

I will leave you with instructions.

I have taken my notes.
I have turned myself inside out with you.
I have let you show me all of your fears.

If I am startled
it was only because
I was a good animal.
I knew the melted mammalian mind
of human skin.
I knew the violence of possession.
But I want to be human.

I want to not be caged.
I want to live outside
of the traverse electric
of your biting retort.

I want to not
lock myself into
your science.
Your mother's expectation.

I wish I did not feed you so easily.
I wish I did not find
all of your allusions so trite.

Send them in again.
Single file.
Chained to the ghosts of men
already greater than them.

I've loved too hard, Dear.
Gutted, stretched, contorted, used
and twisted.

I saw.
Died to see that God
did not love me.
That only Archons
inhabit my periphery.

I cannot play small.
If I die without a lover
I would die happy.

There is nothing you can give me.

This saccharine mammalian.

This act of becoming.
This super imposition.

Nothing gets me drunk enough.

Not like that wine
from that small case we found.
That hidden intoxicant
atop the anemic ladder.

That kind.

12292016

Once you could feel her anger.
Hear her laughter
hot in your own belly.
Echoing off cement walls
of buildings she could have
walked past days ago.

You have lost the sensitivity
to the pulse of her life.
What book does she return to the library.
What shorts does she wear as she walks there.
What band will she see.
Which songs does she play over and over.

You will lose her scent.
Her hair will grow out
and be trimmed.
Grow out
and be trimmed.

You will not know her passion.
What city calls to her
after she makes a home
in the city she has left for.

Soon
the anxiety
of casually bumping into her
among mutual friends will vanish.

Perfect emptiness follows
the threat of her presence.

You will wake from dreaming
of embracing her and feel
no longing,

You will dress to
leave the house without coffee.
During your morning commute
you will remember holding her in a dream.

You will think,
someone can hold her much better now.
Someone can hold her knowing
what thrives within her.
What sets her into bliss.

Instead of a man calling for the ghost
of what she may have been.

Water color impressions
washed out
in the trick of memory.

Woman

I came here to write,
explore, read, and taste.
I came here to burn and be whole
on my own.

I have not come to teach you.
I have not come to heal you.
I am not divinely manifested.
I am not the eternal feminine incarnated
to cosmically yin your yang.

Woman: stolen domestic labor
used to bolster the experiment of capitalism.
Woman: the embodiment of softness
made to teach love to men who
have had the compassion washed out of them.

Do not harm me and call it your divine right.
I cannot be rubble left behind
in the wake of your ignorance.

Sun

He humbles me.

I'm not sure if I want to be with him
or be him.

He inspires me.

I wish that I had a decade
to grow with him.
To explore his mind.
His soul.

He embodies places in me that I hide.

I know him.

The kindest thing I can do
is to be like light.

To remain at a calculated distance.

To titrate the passion
so that we can enjoy each other
without destroying each other.

I pour too much gin on an empty stomach.

I adore him,
He is far.

It Is Not Art

We tend to our lust
hurried by the possibility
that it may age and whither
faster than us.

How will our love perish.
How do good intentions die.
And who knows where they lead.

My verse is flat and dry.

I do not peer beneath
our convincing prose
for fear that the centre
of saccharine pleasantries
melt into hollow core.

No life for coaxing.

I meant to wake you
to say that
this is not love.

I meant to
warn you
that the passions
are too easily misinterpreted.

I shrugged it off.
Rolling back over

to fall dreaming.

I dream that
somehow
someone
somewhere
made me write
in tender fountains.

I dreamed I was
cunningly groomed
into mild vulnerability.

I dreamed I felt
an anchor of trust
that held me in the depth
that I sought to undress.

I dreamed I was
stripped willingly
and that the soft parameters
of our lives
became art.

Gardens growing into hot beds
where stars are nursed.

I woke from that dream
into another
where you slide up close
against my back and ask
what it is like to consume another.

To cling to each syllable

that falls from their lips.

To absorb all of their inspirations.

Once I felt men
move through my arms,
out of my fingers,
and out of my pen.

Once I felt them
ring through my chest
and out of my mouth
in churning melodies.

Once it seemed
that there was
endless nuance to probe
for art and life.

I shunned the muses!
Devoured lover's stories
making them my own.

I meant to wake you.
To tell you that
this is love.
And it is not art.

It does not turn me inside out.
It does not wring joyous salt
from my skin.

I make my own electricity.

We pause
to understand
how lust ages.

How it withers
faster than us.

To witness how love perishes.

Following good intentions
where they lead.

My verse is ordinary.
Love was a noble work.

Maybe as noble as art.

I Do Not Love You Today

I do not love you today.

There are moments
when the macrocosm
sucks me out of the void
my heart gravitates toward.

We don't play a fair game.
My love is too big.
You must make me feel small.

Be preoccupied.
Let yourself be taken
by the sweetness of others.

Be silent until I feel nothing.
Until there is no more chemistry
to be made up.

I do not love you today.
Yet you will ask for me.

Your call is no longer opiate
that I take through thirsty veins.

It is an electric gate
that shocks me back into
solitude.

I do not love you today.

Chiron

What does the static resounding
from the wound as deep as void mean.

Is it a warning or a muffled yawn
as the open sore gasps for breath.

It must mumble sometimes
to keep itself alive.

I do not know what sustains it.

A rush of talk.
A flight of ideas.
I try to decipher
without contextualizing.

Learning to let a thing live
with out qualifying it.
Without reckoning.

It talks out of turn
like an imaginative child.

There is no bandage
for Chiron's open thigh.

Only an ear that listens for sense
in its endless oration.

Orpheo Looks Back

Were you burning for us
in between the deep warm crosscurrents
of blissful veins.

Do you remember the chords
to the song we wrote—
the song that held every sound
I longed to cast upon a crowd.

The notes are now too sweet and thick
for my throat.

There is not enough air in my lungs
to carry those wandering melodies.

I have tried to keep a pulse in the stanza.
I am spinning in the center of the shapes
your fingertips make.

I am bending with your strings.
I am uncovering our shared dream.

If you are only a memory
then I hope that a memory
can be sturdy enough
to keep my passions.

I grow grey and vapid.
I trade the blues for Bach.
I am translating soul into statistics.

I am forever searching
for the sound we make
in the hollows
of drums and guitars.
In the cadence of
mundane conversation.

When I make that sound again
I will be home.

Were you burning for us
in between the deep warm crosscurrents
of blissful veins.

Do you remember the chords
to that song we made.

Crown and Anchor Me

I wanted to wring verse from our complexity.
Bound and clinging like mycelium.
Nothing takes root here.
In suspended pleasantries
of air kisses and hollow sweetness.

I hold my breath and clutch
fleeting anxieties.
Asking to be anchored
or buried.

Exclaiming that I am real
amid scenes
merely requiring the cast
of a woman.

I am only an outline.
Something to be drawn in.

Filled with forward presumption.

He uses soft language
to shade hesitantly
as I long to witness
watercolor flood and saturate
the pages,
transgressing forms.

Silence

FOR AARON CHEAK

I wake into the thought of you
to whisper good morning.
I pull a pillow into my chest
waiting for a third alarm to signal
full alertness.

I caress you gently
with a thought that thinks
that you are the most important thing.

It is not yet time
and you are fast asleep.
A silence on the other side
of the sea.

When the sun reaches mid-sky
I remember to say I love you again.
I remember to tell you that you
are what I want most as you finally rise.

There is a long pause where my love lives.
It is caught in a container called silence
that holds each moment I could not touch you
or console you.

Silence holds every kiss
that would not reach
your mouth or cheek.

My love is held for exhibition
in that transparent jar.

Suspended in emptiness.
In void.
Way out in space
where all mild warmth and passion
collapse.

You are the final sound that I cannot mute
when all of the chatter in my soul ceases.
A sound that is bright as air
and deep as groans
that could be pain or passion.

Love is possession.
Love is selfish
as it devours.
My soul starves for you.

Love cannot be chosen
it is spontaneous
with ravenous hunger.

Gentleness, altruism, selflessness:
words thought to be attainable
by participation in that archaic act
that delivers us closer to nature.
Qualities sought in participation with surrender.

Love, a madness that takes you for its own.
A force that twists rationality until it succumbs
to the will of passions.
Then becomes one with them.

What were you thinking.
Did you hear new phrasings to add
to the prolonged symphony we were writing.
Is it a good work.

You are constantly arriving.
You are ever occurring.
You have never left me.

I want to listen
to the wishes whispered
into our silence.

I want to press my ear against
the void
that holds our story.

Our story
that holds your interiority
and mine at once.

I want to hear the work
that reveals the expanse
and depth of silence.

I want to press my ear
against the soft navel
of the belly
that digests the duality
and complexity
of what our love makes.

Eventually
our daylight ceases
simultaneously.

I kiss you goodnight.
Offering sweetness to silence.

You are constantly arriving.

You are the sound in my soul
that follows the muteness
of every worry.

You have never left me.

You are the sound that permeates darkness.

Catharsis

The wound cannot be written out.
We will not empty ourselves
of self-loathing with language.

Not tonight.
Not this time.
Or ever.

Love was merely an enthusiasm.
Changeable. Quick to sway.

The project made of learning it
a meaningless one.

The ironing out of distortions
smooths the wrinkles of passion
into sterile chrome heaven.

Cold to brushing fingertips
losing their prints
as we forget
to be self-conscious.

I Want To Love You More Than Poetry

I want to love you more than poetry.

I want to surrender to you
like a melody that is warm
and softly perfect.

That melts me entirely.

Our love,
a form of art
that is exquisite.

Miraculously safe.

When He Finds Her

When he finds her
I hope his world stops spinning.

Every portion of taste that she gives him
satiates his hunger for days at a time.

I hope that she is his gravity,
his physics.

I hope he cherishes every grain of sugar
she places on his tongue.

I hope that he desires
nothing, no one less.

How You Are

Today is the first day
that you and I will begin
relinquishing each other
for eternity.

It is nine in the morning.
I know you are just waking
but I cannot greet you like the sun.

Soon we will fumble
through the embers
of smoldered passion
to rest in the safety
of our acceptance.

Finally thinking of you
does not lead me to ask
how you are.

Asking A Stranger

Asking a stranger
to help you see yourself.

So Many Singers

So many singers.

Enough for four thousand choirs.

Was it God under their skins
that made notes emit
from their bellies bright as epiphanies.

Are we all pouring from the same
endless ocean of soul.

What is in us that makes this music.

It turns me inside out.
Moves and rocks my organs
into deep restoration.

Takes me back to source.

So many singers.

So many mother songs
leading us into cosmic intimacy,

Folding us into blankets of constellations.

What did I hear through the open window
of that kitchen
in that second story apartment.

A medicine woman,
a wise man.

Endless jazz and philosophy.

Was it a stranger understanding me.

I Don't Know What To Say

FOR SETH COMBS

I don't know what to say
except that our solitude
becomes more ornate with age.

The harmonies multiply.
The melodies bright and gentle.

I don't know what to say.
Except that hearts will not
merely surrender
once you have succumb
to equanimity.

I have come to see
if I have learned
how to sever unflinching.

I only know how
to remain broken.

I only know how to remain broken.

You come to test the extent
of your concern for compromise.

I stretch love thin.
I extend will into apathy.

I don't know what to say.

Except that your solitude is beautiful.
Our separateness produces its own works.

There is no one I would rather hear
beyond the boundary of heartache.
No one that I would rather hurt.

Your medium sized gilded heart
which at thirty-nine
you have finally unchained.

Your sunken wet tar lungs
which patch notes and stanzas
on command.

I hear your writing your first song
about the emptiness between us.

Of course it is my fault.

I don't know what to say.
When the world
does not open or soften
to your sudden eagerness.

I come to see
if you would show me
how to leave the table
once you are no longer
being served.

I come to run my hand

along the sleek texture
of disdain
and learn to call it justice.

I don't know what to say.
When no one gets their way.

The Brightness

He moonlights in my dreams.
Subsumed by golden vapor
I am amazed how faint memory
feels as convincing as cold marble.
Inhabited by animus.

I say his name out loud.
Mumbling syllables.
Awakening myself with his voice.
Then sink deeper into sleep.

I melt into the bosom
of the man inside of me.

The one that sleeps beside me
asks about the foreign language.
Upon waking I cannot recall.

I only say his name in sleep.
I breathe a soft haze of elation.

Finally, he comes without pain.
Finally, all tangible,
invaluable artifacts.

A decade to misplace shadow.
A decade to feel, at last,
the warm glow of the sun before it sets
and not shiver in shade.

A decade to return to brightness.

Intimacy

Finding I had not wrung the dream out of myself
when I was disappointed by our small fireworks.

I set us on fire.
Enough ash to fill a small earn remained.

If we see each other again
we will not be misled
by visions of the eternal.

One dry night of slight warmth.
A nod to fatality.

Condemned with the failure
of misconstruing the complex
masterwork of intimacy.

Cave

His works terrify me.
I hold them as evidence against him.
They are loved by brutal men.
He must create them.

12072019

I set myself on fire
then scream into the night.
In my ash I called out
for every thing fighting.

Every thing imprisoned.
Every thing kneeling.
Every thing slumbering.

12082019

This is the final time
I shower,
shave,
dye my hair,
wait for you.

When I first saw you
I was convinced
of eternity.

Consumed, mistaking an
identity of discoverer.
I fell endlessly.

I want to stand on my own two feet.

Magdalene

Magdalene
ditched dinner
because everyone
was pronouncing
her name incorrectly.

In The End Everything Is Simple

FOR LEONARD COHEN

Rilke, Rumi, Plath, Lorca
Neruda, Nin.

Stripped down to children's songs
so that they may play us out again.

Songs all dreamed by a manic woman
with a charcoal heart.

In the end
everything is simple.

Each Cell Is A Poem

Wavering goodbye, forgiven,
a secret wish that they will return
in a new form.

We have been healing with theory.
We have healed through sound and notation,
with drugs and some freedoms.

I was not the center.
Merely a conduit.
Harmony and static
body too numb to feel.

Awe in the grandiose and complex.
Tribal liberations
transgressing borders and barriers.

Each cell is a poem.
We have the simple task
of choreography.

Twilight

Waking to him feels like twilight.
He looks stunning
dressing for work in the dawn.

He grows on me.

The hair on his head.

Language is limiting.

Intact

Loyal to the body
which I have punished with perfectionism.
Weighed down with expectation.

I remain in tact.
I wake to myself again.

Thankful that I stretch into corners
of mind feeling into some foreign sanity
or warmth.

I am kind.
I am no longer sick with compassion.

No longer questioning the integrity
of lovers.

Intact.
Loyal to the body.

My Soul Is Hungry For You

My soul is hungry for you.
My soul seeks an unknown purpose through you.
She wants to see through your eyes,
feel with the insides of your palms,
touch with your fingertips.

We are meddling hearts
that know the other
through separation
until spirit transcends and includes
differentiation
for the ego to comprehend
oneness.

Anticipation of depth and span
in our potential chemistry
growing down
into a foundation for flourishing
that shines out through the personality.

Shines out
through reaction and micro expression.
Through the way we tell our stories of creation.
Our stories of the state of things.

A chemistry that turns us inside out.
That becomes transparent through our mediums.

I am sorry that we hide from each other.
I am sorry that you have decided that

we must find each other again
when we are both old,
or when we are both new
in forms I cannot fathom.

I try to keep you by insisting
that there is a song inside you
that only I can learn to sing.

That there are countless potential stanzas
waiting to be brought forth
through our alchemy.

A longing for eternity.
A longing to be present
for the way love
transforms us.

I am moved to flesh out
what insight we lost
by losing each other
before we met in this life.

You wring my heart out
then tell me
that we are the word
brevity.

My Grief Is Not Simple

My grief is not simple.

Wedded to art
yet never deserving her.

I behave like a well-mannered guest.

Guest

FOR ARIEL LEVINE

I kissed him
without guilt.
Fueled by fondness
and clear liquor.

Our bodies moved on beat.
We progressed on two and four
until he paused before the bridge.
Holding time against force.
Never elaborating.

The stammering
made my heart
grow flat.
Leaning past logic
into a parted mouth.

These are the lips
I kiss stiffly in winter.
These are the lips
I suck irreverently in summer.

His face is bare.
He wears all black.
I am looking at him
for the first time
with starved eyes.

We look elegant exiting the bar.

There are no witnesses.
He is following his sleek blazer home.
it's satin lining feels cool
against my bare shoulders.

We are writing our love story
too close to the despair
we caused each other.

I am undressing averse
to the woman he held
against his chest last night.
We are entangled in a chaos
the hunger in our souls satiates,
harmonizes into bearable static.

What is this trust that I feel.
It is warm in my lined palms.
I want to keep him
all night.

I have hurt him before.
I have written callous lines
that painted me stale
in the midst of mistake.
Numb to nuance.
Selfish and brooding.

Concealing disappointment
in song and in conversation.
In hopes that love and boredom
will cause scar tissue to dissolve.

He feels like my favorite verses.

I press into his words and dance gently
with the lines.
The suppleness of poetry.
The structure of logic.

He meets me then
melts into me
before pausing to question
how the ocean never stops
lapping the shore at night.

Sturdy as my favorite poem.
Treacherous
as his deepest regret.

I've mumbled "I love you"
into my pillow
six times since Tuesday.

His cool demeanor
caused two tears
to fall down my thighs.

Is salt and liquid
all that makes us human.
Will our endearment
eventually become cynicism.
Our story unfolds outside of
our respective ideals.

I am afraid that I can destroy this
with a sharp tongue
or syllables bubbling rapidly
in sharp consonants

of erratic vulnerability.

I dream a poem
that gathers all passions
into a drum of stanzas.

I behave like a well mannered guest
anticipating being invited to leave
at any moment.

Dressing A Wound

This is the summer she
gets her first state funded abortion.
The summer she leaves her home of two years.

All of her nightmares come true
before humidity settles into her bones
so that her tears feel cold upon her cheeks.

In this moment
she folds a thick wool blanket
around a fresh wound.

She promises herself
she will unwrap it
once she is forced
to reconsider eternity
for a second occasion.

My Grief Is Sacred

He punches me in the stomach
then tells me how badly it hurt his fist.

If I begin to grieve I may never stop.

Repeated phrases
with intent that
they will bring relief.

My grief is sacred.
It takes its time.

Content In Ordinary Love

I cannot trust my senses
to accurately record.

Will I remember you.

I feel poetry coming to me
as I lie in your arms.

To feel content in ordinary love.
To sink into the monotony of
ever present softness.

Blue Eyed Soul

Everything he made
was a child screaming at god.
Attempting to know him
through tantrum.
Spending his vocal chords
unpacking multitudes of surreal metaphor.
Hurling countless tools and weapons
until he rendered language meaningless.

I cannot soothe him.
I cannot save him from a
Beat poets frenzied pursuance
of the eternal.

"A fool who persists
in his folly
will become wise."

Wailing at the gate of Mysticism
with ornate psalms fashioned
with phrases of Nietzsche, Sartre, Heidegger.
Adrenaline rush of hard consonants too harsh
to achieve the soft heart of a Sufi who effortlessly
unlocks that imaginary door.

Blue eyed soul that discreetly
pierces the narrow vein to heaven
in our shared bathroom
so that I can imagine that I am
what makes him melt into the mattress

beside me.

Mother opiate.
Young enough to let him break me
for a show, for a handful of poems
and electricity.

Everything Now

You are all muscle now.
Where once you merged
with the world in ceremony,
that is only an idea,
a faint prayer that silences chaos
in order to do right loving.

Your pain body reads like brail,
raised scars and burn marks
only visible when the moon is full
and sits in the sky at a perfect angle.

How long ago was it
that you could break like a child.
You were thin glass,
tasting every ripple around you,
easily shattered.

Ashamed at how easily the mind splinters,
and now, feeling shallow and hollow
in a new resilience.

How long ago did you celebrate
and revel in wet paint and ambiguous symbol.
You were comfortable as deindividuated organism
within the great system of art.

One with stanza, one with melody,
one with a distilled spirit.
At the price of feeling everything.

At the price of being mainlined
into grief, shame, guilt,
wonder, ecstasy, fear, beauty.

You are all trunk now
and every gorgeous and terrifying thing
you let inside has crystallized.

You are an ordinary object
with all of the lights turned on inside.

Maps

When you sleep with a man
who does not love you
your skin becomes a weathered map
that is read with a magnifying glass.

Each mark is a river
leading to indifference.
Every freckle a mole.
Your hips once round and soft
become wide and cumbersome.

The love you feel in the morning has been
removed from your chest by afternoon.
Extracted and inspected,
offered to the vacuum that disposes of
the original and the natural.

You become maiden, mother, and crone,
then flatten yourself.

Submitted to the practice
of viewing the self as object.

Heal by turning to familiarity
to what is iridescent within,
and what glows in being unknown.

Discovered You

I feel listless.
Much to do.
Little focus.
A shower helps.

Arrogance.
As if I have discovered you.

Habits

I no longer feel sad.
I have learned the extent
that my heart can hold.
Habits that I am eager to forget.

Lament

He could not hear the hope
as I remained open.
Despair in admitting
that my heart had run out of wisdom
to guide his indifference with grace.

Laments are love letters.
Laments are purposes
asking for guidance
even as I am pulled
into avalanche.

No one could tell me
that the meaning
of that desolation could supply
prognoses of a life
beyond pain.

Willingness to cradle apathy
in both palms, drag it out
to be inspected by a crowd.
Uncovered rage.

Hope rests silent, invisible
as I am limp in his will.

My exhibition is treacherous.
I continue to attempt to explain my heart.
I write alone to synthesize integrity
from fragments of muteness, intention,

half truth.

I wrote alone to construct some form
of silent dignity that might deliver me
from our failure.

Regret for seeking an ear.
Regret for desiring coherence.
Regret for denying my own wholeness.

To be in his good grace
is to be unknown.

Song

There is a time and a place for every song.
I tried to see ours sweetly.

Prometheus

FOR CODY CLARK

We were on fire.
Veins filled with bright hallucinations.
We were digging into the night for insight;
teasing each other as we undressed parts of truth.
We were the mother.
Vehicles bounding through chaos
in pursuit of enlightenment.

We have grown proper.
Learned to be mute in friendship with void.
Intimidated into silence by indifference.
Tamed by etiquette.
Waiting to attend to mortality
to articulate something
heavier than the mundane.
Knowing that even death is mundane
and that our fear will be new.

We had nearly arrived.
Trembling at the mouth of the grotesque,
reflecting the light of complete beauty.
Every symbol too vague to capture with
narrow vocabulary.

I could turn myself inside out like an old t-shirt,
for you. I could count my veins
if it would encourage you.

Every nuance is an abstract symbol

on the map of the soul
that leads us to god.
Every morsel worth devouring
to write one thousand words
describing its taste.

Tell them that we shuffled through the darkness
blindfolded like this.
Toddled through the nocturnal with open palms.
Feeling our way through the work,
while forgetting there was a destination.
Contorted our limbs in the suffocating embrace
of tradition.
Writhing
in the tight arms of a patriarch,
until we were dropped into orphan-hood.

To say you were my muse is too slight.
We were explorers, comrades —
kissed, blistered, by the sun,
filled with light,
messy with earth.

Hosts for parasites who couldn't drive reckless
through the storms we cast ourselves into.
Coveted for the thin veil of consumable beauty
we've learned to hide our ugly souls behind.

You helped me love my fear,
the way you tilted your head back
to laugh into the treacherous night,
baring your teeth to the void.

We were on fire.

Veins filled with bright hallucinations.
We were digging into the night for insight;
teasing each other as we undressed parts of truth.
We were the mother.
Vehicles bounding through chaos
in pursuit of enlightenment.

If you make it back home before I do
tell them that we tried.

Anniversary

Today is our anniversary.
I have spent a year
digging up the roots of our love.
Inspected them.
Gestures you insisted
would cause our death.

I thought I was pruning.
Uprooting in order to replant
in larger earth.

Why?

1)

    a)
    b)
    c)

2)

    a)
    b)
    c)

3)

    a)
    b)
    c)

In This Place

I have realized our failings
were fueled by disease.

Can I love through the hurtle
of our starvation.

Tranform a pattern.

My anguish runs like a thread
through the entirety of life.

I cannot feel.
where my psychosis
and my cognitions
stop and start.

Emotion becomes symptom.

Each place that we do not give love
becomes a growth.

We move within this place.
Dealt with in joy, sorrow, and semen.

What does not flow is dormant.
It hardens with entropy.

Emotions become symptoms

Each place that we do not give love

becomes a growth.

In this place
love is made of
joy, sorrow, and cynicism.

Tell Me

I

Tell me how far away you want me to stand.
I will stand there.

II

I cannot mirror your indifference.

III

There are no such things as good or bad muses.

IV

Show me what it means
to be born on a day that
belongs to the world.

V

I cannot get you on the phone.

There is a place for us.

Tell me that I can be your lover again
before you are taken from that final dream.

What makes us real.
What makes prophets and kings.

Aaron

You become part of the machine
that makes my art.
I am making meaning
of how love can stretch
across continents to you.

Awakened from a half-dream.
Paralyzed by the heaviness of being one.
Awake to feel the trauma of consciousness.
There is an "I" somewhere that exists
where she thrives our oneness is like parasite.

I would rather kill what cannot belong to you
then rip you away from me.

I wake with a growth.
I feed the space where we overlap.
I grieve.

My life takes place in your absence
for years.
You are the most visceral passion
I can know.

To live where no "I" exists.
To do only your work.

I dreamed you.
I dreamed you into every cell
of my bright body.

You were the sun.
I woke to you every morning.
I fell asleep to your voice in my ear.

I watch you die before me.
I let you.

Knowing that I will live without you for decades
I imagine moving openly with your loss
heavy in my heart until my death.

I give you the machine that makes my art.
You, who have moved my pen
each day for three years.

I have convinced myself of your mystery.
I have taken vows in your alchemy.

Good

I hope that the desire to love
without knowing how
makes us good.

Phantom Limb

I add detail to the vibrant images left
conjuring flash bulb memory
grows faint in spiral time.

Finger pointing at the moon.

Cultivate indifference,
dissociation.

Who is succubus
plugging into drain
ardent praise from the one body.

Moonlight bathed us.

My mind pounds under the night sky
vast and ringing with questions
aching manifestations.

Phantom limb.

Transmuting polar emotion.

I use your impressions against myself
one at a time, over and over again.

Heavy

The machine that makes my art
is made of oceans and stars.

Entranced by surface patterns.
Taken by appearances.
I forget to perceive depth.

I count waves in pairs of two
and forget to name constellations.

I am too heavy with why.

Heavy with mystery.

We Are Lived By Everything That We Love

Mexicano-mestizo,
migrating into another
colonizers house of war.
Abuela,
folding her homesickness into
clean pastel sheets.
Churning her might into the maize.
She kisses my cheek
then my forehead
then places the trinity upon my chest
with index and middle finger.
Mijita, she calls me
with bubbling
weeping joy.
My sisters' grandmother,
Afghan refugee
poise with languages we did not speak.
She pressed her craft
into the conjoined corners
of wonton wrappers
then let the steam out
of the pressure cooker
safely before serving.
She does not touch me.
She glances at me with seriousness
making a soft gesture with her strong forearm
across a Persian rug, for her black tea,
set with dates, golden raisins, soft cheese.
Her mind is sharp
her tongue knows

French, German,
Farsi, Dairi,
English.
Joon, she calls my sisters
with a warmth
that is followed by
flat and somber seriousness.
My own mother
blue eyed and still blonde
trapped in a basement
somewhere between
her third and seventh years.
Playing midwife and Artemis
to half siblings
for her coked out father who knew the syntax
of fist, snare, and Marlboro.
She is total tyranny.
Her pain burns in her like a civil war.
She torches the safety of home each Tuesday.
She prefaces her
coarse and erratic
morning stories
with Bebe.
I come from a lineage of woman
who conquered the self.
Who bore man-named
madness to survive.
I know their joy, their care.
their patience with my ignorance,
their patience with the stupidity
of patriarchs.
I protect them by keeping their secrets
but their secrets keep me in tortured
silence.

Everything in me must translate them
in order to be uttered
under moon,
under streetlight,
or unforgiving spotlight.
My own voice is a whisper
that tries to sing in Soprano
when it catches the eternal
or some spirit of synthesized joy.
Mostly, I am serious.
Mostly, I feel righteous.
Mostly, I weep
and I forget to eat.
My sister's grandmothers become my mothers.
My mother's mothers become my mothers.
I hear them en el Barrio.
I hear them on a Subway in New York City.
I hear them in a drawl twenty miles north of the Mason-Dixon.
I straddle the border with both of my strong legs.
My heart unhinges its jaw to swallow Estados Unidos.
My thoughts carry to the Middle East
where all that connects us are stars.
My soul has grown with stories.
My love has become boundless.
My pride waivers as
my sense of justice and wisdom
does their work.
I have prayed them into steam
that rises amongst the crackle of cedar on hot stone
with my only spine rooted in the red desert ground.
I have dreamed them as best I can
and composed works of fullness
when I was not busy with the labors of men.

I stay close to the wound.
I convince myself that I know time.
I convince myself that I know where I am going.
I contextualize the suffering of our lineages;
use them as focal points
rather than anchors.
I pretend that I can infer their her-stories,
their magic,
though they are not written.
With centuries of wisdom lost
I cling to a few phrases.
I believe in their
duty and sorrow.
This makes us whole.
Women teach me that each lover that I take
grants me the grace of their wisdom,
be it; science, prose, or scripture.
Women teach me that we are lived by everything that we love.
Women teach me that everything lives because of our love.

www.ingramcontent.com/pod-product-compliance
Lightning Source LLC
Chambersburg PA
CBHW020735020526
44118CB00033B/719